Learning to read. Reading to learn!

LEVEL ONE Sounding It Out Preschool–Kindergarten
For kids who know their alphabet and are starting to sound out words.

learning sight words • beginning reading • sounding out words

LEVEL TWO Reading with Help Preschool–Grade 1
For kids who know sight words and are learning to sound out new words.

expanding vocabulary • building confidence • sounding out bigger words

LEVEL THREE Independent Reading Grades 1–3
For kids who are beginning to read on their own.

introducing paragraphs • challenging vocabulary • reading for comprehension

LEVEL FOUR Chapters Grades 2–4
For confident readers who enjoy a mixture of images and story.

reading for learning • more complex content • feeding curiosity

Ripley Readers Designed to help kids build their reading skills and confidence at any level, this program offers a variety of fun, entertaining, and unbelievable topics to interest even the most reluctant readers. With stories and information that will spark their curiosity, each book will motivate them to start and keep reading.

Vice President, Licensing & Publishing Amanda Joiner
Editorial Manager Carrie Bolin

Editor Jordie R. Orlando
Writer Korynn Freels
Designer Rose Audette

Published by Ripley Publishing 2019

10 9 8 7 6 5 4 3 2 1

Copyright © 2019 Ripley Publishing

ISBN: 978-1-60991-323-6

No part of this publication may be reproduced in whole or in part, stored in a retrieval system, or transmitted in any form by any means, electronic, mechanical, photocopying, recording, or otherwise, without written permission from the publisher.

For more information regarding permission, contact:
VP Licensing & Publishing
Ripley Entertainment Inc.
7576 Kingspointe Parkway, Suite 188
Orlando, Florida 32819

Email: publishing@ripleys.com
www.ripleys.com/books
Manufactured in China in June 2019.

First Printing

Library of Congress Control Number: 2019942254

PUBLISHER'S NOTE
While every effort has been made to verify the accuracy of the entries in this book, the Publisher cannot be held responsible for any errors contained in the work. They would be glad to receive any information from readers.

PHOTO CREDITS

Cover © Fer Gregory/Shutterstock.com; **Master graphics** © A_KUDR/Shutterstock.com; **3** © Fer Gregory/Shutterstock.com; **4-5** © Simon Bratt/Shutterstock.com; **6-7** © SeventyFour/Shutterstock.com; **8-9** © Tom Wang/Shutterstock.com; **10-11** © Olga_Kuzmina/Shutterstock.com; **12** © Linda Armstrong/Shutterstock.c **13** © phloxii/Shutterstock.com; **14-15** © Evgeny Atamanenko/Shutterstock.com; **16-17** © Jeremy Warner/Shutterstock.com; **18-19** © Pictureguy/Shutterstock.com; **20-21** © Piotr Krzeslak/Shutterstock.com; **22-23** (bkg) © Drew McArthur/Shutterstock.com; **22** © Avillfoto/Shutterstock.com; **24-25** © Minerva Studio Shutterstock.com; **26-27** © Jaromir Chalabala/Shutterstock.com; **28** © PixieMe/Shutterstock.com; **29** © M Tagirova/Shutterstock.com; **30-31** © Ami Parikh/Shutterstock.com

Key: t = top, b = bottom, c = center, l = left, r = right, sp = single page, dp = double page, bkg = background

All other photos are from Ripley Entertainment Inc.

Every attempt has been made to acknowledge correctly and contact copyright holders, and we apologiz advance for any unintentional errors or omissions, which will be corrected in future editions.

LEXILE®, LEXILE FRAMEWORK® , LEXILE ANALYZER®, the LEXILE® logo and POWERV® are trademarks of MetaMetrics, Inc., and are registered in the United States and abroad. The trademar and names of other companies and products mentioned herein are the property of their respective owners. Copyright © 2019 MetaMetrics, Inc. All rights reserved.

Ripley Readers

Weather

All true and unbelievable!

a Jim Pattison Company

Sun. Snow. Rain. Wind.

There are so many kinds of weather!

Sunny days are fun days!

The sun can make the weather hot and dry.

Wind is when the air moves fast.

It can help you fly a kite!

Clouds are big and white.

You can look for a cloud that is a funny shape!

Rain comes down from the clouds.

Do you want to jump in a rain puddle?

Oh no! Too much rain will make a flood.

A car cannot go when the road is under water!

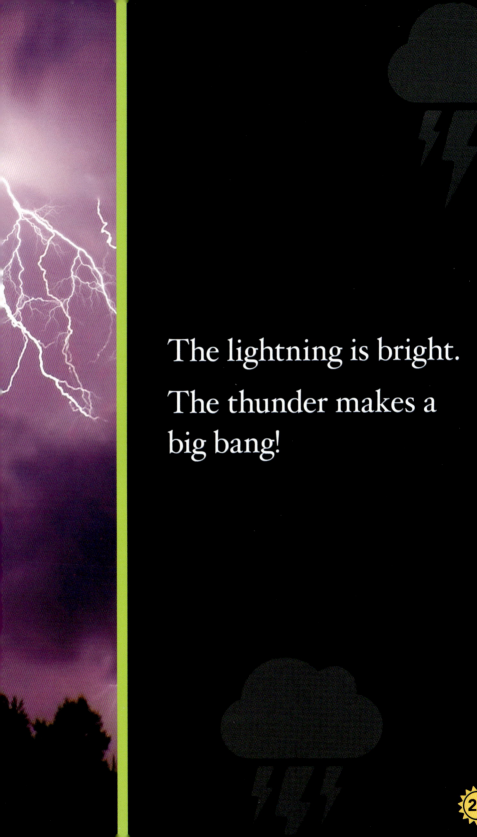

The lightning is bright.

The thunder makes a big bang!

A hurricane is a big storm with lots of rain and wind.

It can make big things fall over.

Wind from a storm can spin fast to make a tornado!

Fog is a cloud
so low you can
walk in it.

Fog can make it
hard to see.

Snow is made of little flakes.

No two are the same.

Snow is cold, but it is fun to play in!

Ripley Readers

All true and unbelievable!

Ready for More?

Ripley Readers feature unbelievable but true facts and stories!

   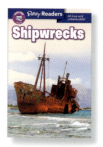

Look for Ripley Readers on Amazon.com!